WRANGLE ON CAPITAL PUNISHMENT

VOLUME 2, ISSUE 3 OF BRILLOPEDIA

N R BRIJESH

Contents

Preface

"Start writing, no matter what. The water does not flow until the faucet is turned on".

• Louis L'Amour

Hundreds of students and professors are contributing their work to Brillopedia, we are here to provide ample information about Law and Contemporary issues. Our aim is to provide a platform for today's generation to express their views and ideas on law and contemporary law.

Publication

This research paper is published in volume 2, issue 3 of Brillopedia

Author

N R Brijesh

ABSTRACT

This paper critically discusses the presence of capital punishment from the philosopher's point of view. Capital punishment is the process of sentencing a convicted offender to death for the severe crime or wrongful act that they have performed and carrying out that sentence. The practice of capital punishment was first introduced by the European settles in the year 1608. Although countries like Brazil, Denmark, Norway, and Luxembourg have abolished capital punishment, around sixty percentage of the world's population live in countries which still have the practice of capital punishment. Different philosophers have their own views and the practice of capital punishment. Aristotle's suggest that he was against the practice of capital punishment. Whereas, St Thomas was a vocal supporter of capital punishment. St Thomas theory states that the State not only have the right but it is also the duty of the state to protect people from enemies. The different theories of punishments also have different opinions on capital punishment. The retributive theory in its simplest form propagates the idea of "An eye for an eye". It gives importance to individuals more than state. It believes in the practice of reformation and rehabilitation. The deterrence theory gives more importance to the society more than an individual. It believes that punishing an individual is morally correct if it brings a considerable change to the society. Both utilitarians and deontologists have the opinion that punishments are justifiable. Having critically analyzed the opinions of different philosophers and theories, this paper tries to make an attempt to bring an end to this debate.

INTRODUCTION

The term Capital punishment is a Latin term meaning "Capitalis" which means "regarding the Head." Capital punishment is the process of sentencing a convicted offender to death for the severe crime or wrongful act that they have performed and carrying out that sentence. The practice of Capital punishment is being followed from a long period of time. It was first introduced by the European settlers in the year 1608. It is been followed in many countries including India.It is carried out in a variety of ways, including the guillotine, hanging, lethal injection, electrocution, firing squad, and so on. The execution is not always carried out immediately. Their names are kept on the death row for a time while their cases are appealed. In some cases of lesser offences, an appeal for life imprisonment is possible. In this paper I have critically analyzed different views of the philosophers on capital punishment and tried to end the debate on the justification of capital punishment.

ARISTOTLE

Aristotle was against the practice of capital punishment. According to Aristotle justice means giving people what they deserve and it requires things to be given to people equally. Aristotle believes that everyone wants to be a good human being based on naturalism and self-realization. He believed that human beings would revert to natural tendencies in order to achieve their own happiness. Natural tendencies for good character evolve over time and through practice. In other words, no one is born perfect, and everyone has the same chance of committing immoral acts as they do of performing good deeds. The habits that a person develops over time shape their personality during the ups and downs of the vicious cycle of moral or immoral decision-making. This defines a person's virtue in terms of how well they deal with the vicious cycle. Aristotle believed that the natural state of pleasure was neither good nor bad, but rather a natural byproduct of developing good character. [1]This is an intriguing concept in terms of immoral acts of violence that some may find pleasurable to commit. One might arguethe mental state in which such acts are committed Regardless, does it make it right for society to decide morality in the form of justice for that person?

[1]Aristotle's View on Capital Punishment (2005 October 14)

THOMAS AQUINAS

Thomas Aquinas defends the right to execute, that is capital punishment. The death penalty, like other punishments, is a decision made by human reason. Its justification depends on specific historical and cultural circumstances and on the needs of the political community, as well as on the severity of the offense. Killing a guilty person is not intrinsically evil, in Aquinas's view, but it is nonetheless a last resort, when nothing else can be done for the good of the community.[1] Thomas defends capital punishments on medical grounds. He sees the community as patient. For punishment is not always meant to be medicine for a single offender; sometimes the "patient" is the community. The goal of capital punishment is to benefit the community rather than the offender. Aquinas says that capital punishment should be used where it is useful to the common good and in accordance with human custom, but it should not be used where it is not useful to the common good and is not in accordance with custom.

[1] Saint Thomas Aquinas on the Death Penalty Author: Elinor Gardner

JEREMY BENTHAM

Jeremy Bentham was the founder of utilitarianism. According to him punishment is considered to evil because it causes some pain and suffering. But, punishment can be permitted on utilitarian ground if it is done for the greater good of the people and it prevents some greater evil. So according to Bentham punishment is to prevent crime in order to secure the greatest good for the greatest number. Jeremey Bentham supports capital punishment it will promote the happiness of greatest good for the greatest number in the society. According to him, capital punishment is justifiable is it is able deter crime and reform criminals. Capital punishment can serve as an effective measure for serious crimes as it prevents people from committing crimes and it will also act as a tool to satisfy people. But there are also some problems associated with implementing capital punishment. One of the problems associated with capital punishment is that capital punishment can be mistakenly carried out on innocent victims. Many people have been proclaimed to be innocent long after the execution. This radical form of execution is carried out in some cases against the poor and people from low economic situation or background.[1]

I personally believe that Capital punishment is required for this society. The society in which we live in has a lot of wrong doers who are not guilty of it. According to me, people should be sentenced to capital punishment who repeat the same mistake again and again. Capital punishment puts in a sense of fear to all the wrong doers who will fear to commit the same mistake again. I also feel that there should be stricter rules and regulations to be imposed and it should be implemented properly. The main aim of capital punishment is to make sure that common people live peacefully and to reform the other wrongdoers.

I am a strong believer of utilitarian theory proposed by Jeremy Bentham and would state utilitarian theory as a defense for capital punishment. The happiness of the greatest number of people in the society matters the most. In a democratic country like India the happiness or peacefulness of people is important. Talking about democracy I also feel that Monarch would be a better way of governance in India because most of the people in India gets easily carried away by political parties and those parties use the common people to satisfy their needs. I also feel that the sanction on the politicians who commit wrong should be stricter, which in itself will help to the development of the country.

There are also some shortcomings of capital punishment. If the execution of capital punishment is liberalized people tend to take advantage of it. People will have no fear of committing offense or crime again and again which will increase the crime rate. If this is done, the powerful will oppress the powerless. People who will have power (in terms of wealth, politics etc.,) will have an edge over those who does not have power.

[1]Epistemic Investigation into Jeremy Bentham's Theory of Capital Punishment

CONCLUSION

Having analyzed the point of view of different philosophers I personally feel that capital punishment is necessary but there has to be certain conditions in executing it. People who commit grievous offences will have to be executed. It is only when we can prevent others from doing it and can move towards a crime less society.

PAUL VS. STATE OF KERALA

VOLUME 2, ISSUE 2 OF BRILLOPEDIA

MRIDULA SHANKER

Contents

Preface

"Start writing, no matter what. The water does not flow until the faucet is turned on".

-Louis L'Amour

Hundreds of students and professors are contributing their work to Brillopedia, we are here to provide ample information about Law and Contemporary issues. Our aim is to provide a platform for today's generation to express their views and ideas on law and contemporary law.

Author

Mridula Shanker

Abstract

In this paper, the case of **Paul v. State of Kerala** is examined in detail. In the present case the prosecution is the brother of the deceased. He claimed that the appellant had been abusive to her sister physically and mentally ever since their marriage. In contrast, the prosecution claimed that it was a suicide. The learned Principal Sessions Judge held the appellant guilty because it was found that the deceased's death was the direct outcome of blunt force applied on the neck, and also there were other marks on the deceased's body that make it abundantly clear that this is not a case of suicide.

Facts

- On the 31st of August, 1997, the appellant married Jessy.
- On the tragic day of 11.10.1998, the appellant's mother caused a commotion in their house.
- The deceased, who was depressed, left the house in search of her husband after being subjected to severe harassment, and found him drinking with his friends.
- The appellant attacked his wife in front of his friends.
- Thereafter, on the same night at about 11.00, the appellant throttled her to death.
- Marks of physical violence were present on the body of the deceased.
- The appellant and his mother were charged with cruelty and causing the death of the appellant's wife under Sections 498-A and 302 read with Section 34 of the Indian Penal Code, but were acquitted. Following that, the appellant's mother died.
- However, in a judgment dated March 29, 2012, a Division Bench of the Kerala High Court allowed the State's criminal appeal against the acquittal and set aside the acquittal insofar as it related to the appellant, remanding the case with a direction to dispose of the case by continuing proceedings from the stage of examination under Section 313 Crpc.
- Following the remand, the appellant was found guilty under Section 302 of the IPC by the Principal Sessions Judge, Ernakulum.
- The Appellant was dissatisfied with the judgment and filed an appeal against the principal session judge's decision.

Issues

i. Is the fact that the Appellant has been injured sufficient to justify the case being moved from section 302 to section 304 part II of the IPC?

ii. When does section 304 of IPC applies and whether it is applicable in this case?

iii. Whether or not the appellant is entitled to get the benefit of exception 4 to section 300 of IPC?

iv. Whether or not the appellant is entitled to get the benefit of exception 1 to section 300 of IPC?

v. Did Jessy commit suicide?

Contention from both the side

Prosecution

- According to the prosecution, Jessy has been exposed to physical and mental mistreatment in the hands of appellant and his mother since their marriage.
- On the tragic day of 11.10.1998, the appellant's mother made a scene at their house.
- The deceased, who was sad as a result of the harassment, left the house in search of her husband and spotted him drinking with his friends.
- The appellant assaulted his wife in front of his friends.
- The appellant then throttled her to death at 11 p.m. on the same night.

Defence

- A quarrel broke between his mother and his wife.
- He got up early in the morning to urinate, and it was only then, he noticed the deceased hanging from the window railings by a shawl and on his crying PW 2 and 3 came to his room.
- They untied the shawl and the body of Jessy was laid on the bed.
- The appellant's counsel requested that the conviction be changed from section 302 of the IPC to section 304 part II of the IPC, citing the fact that the appellant was also injured.

Cases/Authorities Cited

The cases cited were **Pratap Singh vs. State of UP,** Where it was ruled that even if the accused failed to establish his plea, the benefit of the right of private defence cannot reasonably be ruled out from prosecution evidence in a case where the prosecution has not established its case beyond reasonable doubt against the appellant on an essential ingredient of the offence of murder. Also in the case Periasami and Another vs. State of Tamil Nadu, It was established that the law entitles the appellants to the benefit of reasonable doubt. Also the case **State of UP vs. Lakhmi** were referred to where it was ruled that "If an accused admits to any incriminating situation that appears in evidence against him, there is no reason to disregard those confessions just because they were made as part of a defence strategy." Other cases referred to were **Basdev vs. state of Pepsu and State of Andhra Pradesh v. Rayavarapu Punnayya and Another.** The authorities cited in this case were learned principal session judge, "Ernakulum", Division bench of the Kerala High court, K.M. Joseph , Mohan M. Shantanagoudar , Subbarao, J. and Sanjay Kishan Kaul.

Analysis

- There is a case to be made by the appellant that he was injured. It should be noted that unless the victim is sleeping or unconscious, there will be resistance to throttling. It is not uncommon for the aggressor to sustain injuries. Apart from the neck, other areas of the body were also injured in this case. They denote the aggressor's actions of violence. We are not even asked to comment on whether or not there is anyone else who would be the aggressor in this situation as appellant himself confessed that on the fateful night he and his wife were alone in the bedroom. The appellant, and only the appellant, is responsible for the conduct that resulted in his wife's death.

- Exception I to section 300 of the IPC requires the accused to be deprived of his or her power of control as a result of grave and sudden provocation. In this case, there is no evidence to even faintly imply that the appellant was provoked since, according to the prosecution's argument, the appellant's mother set up a scenario that compelled the deceased to leave the house and look for her husband. There is further talk of the appellant mistreating his wife in front of his friends, and then the appellant throttling her in the middle of the night, this clearly shows that there was a time gap between the provocation and the happening of the event.

- Even exemption 4 to section 300 of the IPC does not apply in this case since there is no evidence to support the finding that a sudden dispute led to a sudden fight based on the appellant's assertion in his written statement that he fell fast asleep.

- It was held by the court in State of **Andhra Pradesh vs. Rayavarapu Punnayya**, that Section 304 of IPC applies only in cases where culpable homicide is not murder, and that if the act amounting to culpable homicide meets any of the four criteria that would bring it under the offence of murder, there would be no reason to allow Section 304 to come into play.

- In this case, section 304 of the IPC cannot be invoked because it is clearly evident that the appellant performed the act that resulted in the death. Given the facts of this case, particularly the injuries sustained, it is apparent that the conduct would fall under the purview of Section 300 of the IPC.

- The death was discovered to be an instantaneous outcome of the blunt force delivered to the deceased's neck. PW1 saw marks of physical assault on the deceased's body. The learned Judge then noted the swelling in the middle of the forehead, as well as an abrasion on the left cheek, which were both mentioned in the inquest report. The dead body's nail clippings and blood samples were collected. The appellant's nail clippings were also taken. Blood in nail clippings, according to the appellant, was caused by an attempt by the dead and the appellant to undo the noose around her neck. However, the court did observe, that PW14's doctor stated that once the ligature was fastened around her neck, the victim would become comatose and unable to move her upper limbs to release it. The Court further observed that according to the written statement provided after remand under 313 Crpc, PW1 and PW3, appellant's brothers, untied the shawl said to have been used by the deceased for committing suicide. This clearly shows thatthe version sought to be introduced in the written statement that there was a fight between his mother and his wife on the date of the incident, during which he was also assaulted by his mother, looks like an embellished version and unacceptable because the incident occurred in the appellant's bedroom, at night, with no other person present. This clearly shows that the appellant is guilty of murder by throttling and that the theory of suicide is unacceptable.

Judgment

The High Court upheld the judgment of the learned Principal Sessions Judge, Ernakulum, who found the appellant guilty under section 302 of the Indian Penal Code (for short "IPC") and sentenced him to life imprisonment and a fine of Rs.10, 000/- because the appellant's actions clearly show that he throttled his wife. None of the exceptions listed in Section 300 are applicable. According to Section 300 of the IPC, the conduct amounts to murder.